Other Books by Catherine E. Goin

Mercy, Lord, Mercy

A Broken-hearted Schizophrenic

Spirit of a Sound Mind

CAT Meows 2 by Cat. E. Goin

Changes Deranges

a memoir of sorts

Catherine E. Goin

WESTBOW
PRESS®
A DIVISION OF THOMAS NELSON
& ZONDERVAN

This book is a work of non-fiction. Unless otherwise noted, the author
and the publisher make no explicit guarantees as to the accuracy of
the information contained in this book and in some cases, names of
people and places have been altered to protect their privacy.

WestBow Press books may be ordered through booksellers or by contacting:

WestBow Press
A Division of Thomas Nelson & Zondervan
1663 Liberty Drive
Bloomington, IN 47403
www.westbowpress.com
1 (866) 928-1240

Because of the dynamic nature of the Internet, any web addresses or
links contained in this book may have changed since publication and
may no longer be valid. The views expressed in this work are solely those
of the author and do not necessarily reflect the views of the publisher,
and the publisher hereby disclaims any responsibility for them.

Any people depicted in stock imagery provided by Getty Images are
models, and such images are being used for illustrative purposes only.
Certain stock imagery © Getty Images.

Interior Image Credit: Catherine E. Goin and Adrienne Payette

Scripture taken from the King James Version of the Bible.

ISBN: 978-1-9736-7730-7 (sc)
ISBN: 978-1-9736-7732-1 (hc)
ISBN: 978-1-9736-7731-4 (e)

Library of Congress Control Number: 2019916550

Print information available on the last page.

WestBow Press rev. date: 10/17/2019

Acknowledgments

Catherine Goin for her drawings and cover art

My brother, Russell Goin, without whose help this book would not be possible.

Cynthia Rafala for her encouragement and help in understanding relationships and mental health.

Dr. David Goldstein for his help in the development of creativity, mental and physical well-being.

I will extol thee, O Lord; for You have lifted me up, and have not let my foes rejoice over me.

O Lord my God, I cried to You, and You healed me.

O Lord, You have brought my soul up from the grave; You have kept me alive, that I should not go down to the pit ...

You have turned for me my mourning into dancing: You have put off my sackcloth, and clothed me with gladness:

To the end that my glory may sing praise to You and not be silent. O Lord my God, I will give thanks to You forever.

—Psalm 30: 1–4; 11–12 NKJV

God says,

I must say

    Her life appears a mess,-

A real-live maiden

    In distress.

Unless I choose

    To get involved,

It is unlikely

    Her problem will be solved.

I say,

The doctor said I must be fed,

Unless, instead, I wish to be dead.

I thought about this;

It is quite a twist.

He says I must work hard

To gain some lard.

I do not want to jump

And land with a thump.

I wish, indeed, to live awhile.

And most important,

Do it in style.

God says,

Right on, kid, I dig your spirit.

So big.

Eat with my blessing;

It takes out the guessing

On how to gain weight.

To be thin is not your fate.

I say,

Gracious me, I do declare

I have nothing to wear!

My hospital wardrobe is small.

I hardly have anything at all

In my size.

I continue,

Oh, God, most wise,

You know that talking with God

Seems a little odd.

God then says,

Talking with you

Seems peculiar too.

Contents

So Cool

Many people have been good to me, and I would like to thank them with my words written over many years celebrating the good and the bad, both leading to where I am today, starting many years ago when I was young and living in a small town in a rural community. Having no land on which to raise animals so as to participate in 4H, I took to entomology and became good at it, leaving me with a love of butterflies, beetles, moths, bugs ... ... even spiders unless they are poisonous. I also developed a love for squirrels, cats, dogs, groundhogs, bears, rabbits, foxes, coyotes, and even the occasional nonpoisonous snake. Not to mention the many types of lovely birds and their songs, which brighten up the morning when I take my morning constitutional. So here goes.

Butterfly, Butterfly

Butterfly, butterfly,
 that's my song.
I chase moonbeams
 all day long.

I run toward this,
I run toward that.
I go running in circles.
 Whee!
But running in circles—whee—
gives you time to catch up with me.

But,
if you'd like to catch me
because you like my pretty wings,
remember they're easily broken,
very fragile things.

So be careful!

The Buzzard Bounce

Swooping,
swirling
through the sky,
the big, black buzzards go flying by.

But when it's dinnertime on the farm
and the sky rings out with the buzzard alarm,
then they gather, the buzzards all,
and down through the sky they begin to fall;
they march into the dining hall.

When they've finished, have had their fill,
they march back out, begin to sing and shout,
and do the buzzard bounce.
They flap their wings, they flap their tails,
they throw back their heads, and do the buzzard wail.
All night long the festivities reign,
'til morning comes, and it's time to fly again.
So slowly, slowly they circle up,
'til swooping, swirling through the sky,
the big black buzzards
go flying by, go flying by, go flying by.

Not only nature intrigued me. I had a highly
developed imagination. Was that because I was
creative or because I was traumatized?

The Rock-and-Roll Dragons

Rock and rolling through the night,
the dragons danced away.
They had come from miles around
to sing and dance and play.
The rock-and-roll band
dressed so grand in colors of every hue,
red, pink, yellow, and gold,
silver and green and blue.
With rings in their ears and feathers in their tails,
they banged their drums; their guitars they strummed
as they wailed the latest tunes.

A visiting dragon from out of town,
dressed in traditional green,
smoked a lot—fire, not pot—
as he gazed upon the scene.

Matilda the dragon, a notorious flirt
dressed in her most sensuous scales,
slithered and slid around the floor
and tantalized all the males.

A calico dragon and a red one with one black eye
gamboled and frolicked amidst the uproar.
To be sure, their feet will be sore.
To be sure, their feet will be sore.

A chubby dragon made his way
to the refreshment table, heavily laden.
He rolled back his eyes, shook his scales, and sighed,
"By God, I think I've gone to heaven."

The trees all rocked, the rocks they rolled
as through the forest the dragons strolled.
The moon shone down with all its might,
amazed at such a wondrous sight
'cause normally, dragons love to fight.

All night long the party did last,
'til the sun arose and broke up the blast.

But do not panic; have no fear.
The dragons will gather every year.
They will dance, and they will play
throughout the night 'til break of day.

It is common in most households in the world, rich
or poor, to hate having rats and mice in the house.
This is one reason a lot of people like to have cats.
Cats like to play with and eat mice; it's the law of
the jungle. This is an eventful night in the life of my
favorite cat at the time, Yahu.

Yahu and the Mousies

Around the corner the kitty peaked.
"Oh, good grief," the mousies squeaked.
"Howdy, mousies. My name is Yahu.
"Howdy do?"
"I think you'd better scat.
Discretion is where it's at.
When I prowl, you should hear me growl.
Look at my teeth.
Perfect for little mousies to eat!"

Look at Yahu, the mousies thought.
I guess we ought to scat.
Discretion is where it's at!

Yahu said, "Little mousies on the run.
Oh, boy, this should be fun."
1, 2, 3, 4, hear the kitty roar
as the mousies scamper across the floor
to the mouse-hole in the next room.
If they're not fast, Yahu will be their doom.

Ho, ho, ho, hi, hi, hi.
Across the room the mousies fly.
For them it's either do or die.
Watch the mousies fly.
Into the mousehole they flew.
In hot pursuit was Yahu.
The mousies made it to their hole.
Oh well, thought Yahu, *they got away.*
Tomorrow maybe again we can play.

Filene the Fish

Filene the fish with silver scales
gamboled and frolicked with the whales.
Below the surface of the sunlit sea she lived.
She was wild and free!
She breathed through her gills.
She took no pills.
Plankton was her favorite dish.
She loved being a fish.

Dandelions

Dandelions are here.
Winter is past!
When dandelions come,
it's spring at last!

Spring Poem: The Appearance of Tiger Lilies

Up, up above the ground
they poked their leaves,
looked around.
"Ah," they sigh, "spring at last
The bitter cold of winter is past!"

Ode to Spring

Hippity-hop.
It's spring, and I cannot stop
watching little rabbits hop.
Flippity-flop.
Spring has come, and out of the ground
little daffodils pop!

Little birdies taking a bath
really, truly make me laugh.
The mockingbirds come back in force.
Cat merrily chases them of course.

Earthworms painted shades of brown
go wiggling up, go wiggling down.
They go tunneling through the ground.

Lightning flashes in the air.
Thunder is heard everywhere.
Hippity-hop, flippity-flop.
Even spring poems must come to a stop.
So this is the end, my friend.

Hi

Have a purrfect day.
The day spent with you was superfine.
We must do it again sometime.
You are a splendifurous host, the most.
The camellias were dandy.
Now I'd like some chocolate candy.
The catnip is to sow.
Your friends with cats will love you
When it begins to grow.

The Stars

The stars twinkling on a cloudless winter night.
What a sight!
Constellations boggle my mind.
There are about half a dozen I can find.

It's Hard to Be Sad

It's hard to be sad; it's hard to be mad
when you are glad that spring has come,
and winter has gone.
A tubby robin returning from the South
has a big, fat earthworm in his mouth.
The squirrels raise their voices in one accord,
"Thank You, thank You, thank You,
Lord!"
Now we see the daffodillies,
Soon to be charmed by the tiger lilies!

The Last Day of Autumn

Drip, drip, drip, watch the rain slip
down, down, down upon the ground.
The flowers raise their petals and dance with glee.
They've done this throughout history.
The storm popped out from behind the trees,
propelled by the evening breeze.
Raindrops hit the ground, a mysterious sound.
The sky a tumultuous gray, the winds howled.
The leaves flittered, the leaves skittered.
Leaves flutter from on high, lighting up the morning sky.
My neighbors, all armed with their rakes,
remove them fallen from their place.
Winter is soon to reappear as it does every year.

The Jungle Fight

In the jungle, the plants and trees are green,
variegated shades of green.
Plants climbing, crawling around the trees,
home for snakes, lizards, butterflies, bees.

Louis the lion, one moonlit night,
sauntered across the veld, looking for a fight.
Louis was fast, he was trim, no stopping him.
He howled and growled
as across the jungle he prowled.

Peter the panther, black and sleek,
loved to eat the meek.
Peter was cattin' and slinkin' around,
when through the night he heard a sound.
"What was that? I must know!"
He stood there listening with his eyes aglow.
It was the cry of buzzards and vultures flying by,
circling up in the sky.
Hoping there would be a kill, so they could eat meat.
Have their fill.
The big birds knew the two big cats, so sleek and mean,
were veritable fighting machines.
Louis, so fine in his coat of yellow, was a gorgeous fellow.
Peter, with his dark, dark hide, was content and satisfied.
The monkeys chattering in the trees
were enjoying the evening breeze,
throwing coconuts at the giraffe below.

The skinny giraffe with the long, long neck
was thinking, *Why are they doing this?*
Being harassed by the monkeys was making her a nervous wreck.
She remembered they, the monkeys, liked to play.
That's why they were throwing coconuts her way.

A zebra dressed in white and black trotted across the veld.
He was svelte.
Hunters would love to skin him for a belt.

The animals gathered round to watch the fight, a glorious sight.
Who would win this night?
The moon was sparkling in the sky above,
sending down its twinkling beams,
filling the animals below with dreams.

At last the animals settled down.
The fight did begin; who would win?
Louis and Peter hollered and roared.
Throughout the jungle, their voices soared.
A good fight everyone adored.
Certainly no one would be bored.
Louis tossed his mane, Peter flipped his tail,
they pawed the ground, they circled round.
They hit, they spit, they threw a fit
and hurt each other not a bit.

They got into a tangle.
Everyone's nerves were a jangle.
A fight so fine, a fight sublime.
Finally, the two had enough
They liked to fight but not too rough.
They were kings of the jungle but not too tough.

At last the two cats headed home,
waiting for the next chance to roam,
waiting for the next night to fight,
underneath the sparkling moon and twinkling stars,
under the reddish light of Mars.
Everyone agreed it was a stupendous brawl
totally enjoyed by all.

Not Your Style

"Let's march to the White House and parade there a bit, and then we can go home."
"Wow, did you see all the cops? You would think we were going to riot. Talk about paranoid."
Then off they took— clop, clop, clop.
All the pedestrians did stop.
What is it that the signs do say
As they parade along the way?
I would like to join the march, you know,
although it is going way too slow.
The marchers are dressed just right
for demonstrating on such a lovely night.
Their signs are ac-cu-rat!
At demonstrating, they are old hat.

There were a lot of people from out of town, including a group from Berkeley, California, in the forefront of fashion in their tie-dyed T-shirts, fringed jeans, and Frye boots. I started to feel conservative and insecure, always unsure of myself when dressed inappropriately.

"Simmer down. You look just fine. Where is your self-confidence?" said Mel, who knew of my insecurity. "You are not a hippie. You never will be. It is not your style."

This is the end of the beginning. There is much more, but I can't remember so well. I remember there was dance—modern dance—and a whole lot of music that continued throughout my life. It included the piano, flute, guitar, mandolin, and even attempts are claw-hammer banjo. There was also an effort to learn to play the dulcimer. Unfortunately, I forgot God, and thus begins the sadder part of my story. Not a very pretty story until the latter years, when I remembered about God and why life is full of purpose and meaning.

A Fool

For fourteen years, I courted disaster, living in Williamsburg, Chicago, Seattle, Washington DC, Los Angeles, Honolulu, and San Francisco. I was totally divorced from good sense, living a life of adventure but not happy. "Why?" you ask. Well, read on.

A Fool

When I went to school, I became a fool.
Here's what I heard, word for word.

"God is dead," they said. "God is dead," I read
in Philosophy 101.
Absolute truth is no more, to be sure!
Relativity was the rant; so said Camus, Sartre, Kant.
I fell really hard—hook, line, and sinker—
fancying myself as an advanced thinker.
It was a tumultuous era;
sanity for me didn't have a prayer.
"Boys were toys," was my belief.
Learning they were human
brought me humongous relief.
Going to church became such a bore.
What would I go there for?
I had no rock on which to stand.
My life wobbled round on shifting sand.
Life definitely wasn't grand.
Was God dead? Where did he go?
Does anybody know?

So I became a flight attendant, which was the great
love of my life. I loved planes and being high in
the sky.

Sort of a Sonnet

Airplanes were bouncing throughout the night sky.
Men were all praying, and babies did cry.
Women were scared that their hair was a mess;
this was a reason that made them distress.
The stars in the sky bounced up and bounced down.
Stars seemed to whirl and to twirl all around.
The employees who were usually cool
yelled and cried loudly as they were afraid.
"My goodness gracious," the pilots did shriek.
Frantically through the sky they did seek
air that was stable, kind to the plane.
"My goodness gracious," they said, "We see rain."
The moral it is, if one there should be,
is try to avoid bumps whilst o'er the sea.

At Night on the Plane

After properly introducing ourselves, we three young flight attendants sat in the front lounge of the DC-8 at the lounge table and whiled away the time playing cards, eating caviar, and singing.

Oh, mighty sturgeon from the Caspian Sea,
we love thy roe, thy eggs love we.
Sitting so black on the crispy bread,
while sipping champagne it goes to our heads.
Some prefer vodka; we do not really care.
Both make people happy, we do declare.
For purists like we, the roe alone is just fine.
We arrange it on toast in a straight little line.
Others like egg yolk and white crumbled in bits,
and a touch of onion as it passes the lips.
Oh, caviar, caviar, food of the gods,
we are happy to eat it though we are but clods.
Some think it too salty but certainly not we!
We love you, oh sturgeon, from the Caspian Sea.

We love you,
we love you,
we love you,
do we!

Aloha!

Stars were twinkling when all of a sudden, there were lights down below. We were approaching Honolulu. The captain came over the PA with the following announcement.

Well folks, we are approaching Honolulu.
Fasten your seat belts.
Land is not far away; your trip is ending for today.
We have traversed the Pacific Ocean
With nary a bump caused by turbulent motion.
We are heading for our landing spot in Honolulu,
Where the weather is hot,
Where the balmy breezes blow,
Where there is lava and not much snow.
So aloha from me to you and on behalf
Of the rest of the crew.

It had been a glorious flight, and it was over this wonderful night.

Bouncing over the Sea

Bouncing and bumping over the crashing waves,
bound for watery graves.
We should be tasty dishes
for all the hungry little fishes.

Gliding by so gray and sleek
was a thin-looking shark
who had not eaten for a week.
He said, as my father used to say,
"It's been so long since I've been fed,
my stomach thinks my teeth are dead."
The humans above were all screaming.
"We must be dreaming,"
said the assembled fishes and shark.
"Dinnertime should be a lark.
There are blonds, brunettes, and local boys.
A fine, fine dinner, one filled with joys."

The Banana Patch

Peacefully strolling through the night,
hoping there wouldn't be a fight,
listening to the Dreadful Heads
who got that way by swallowing reds.
Denny and I were ready for a party,
hoping refreshments would be hearty.
Dressed to kill, we hoped to eat our fill,
then sing and dance, no romance.

Bam, bam, bam went the jungle drums.
"Come to the party; from all corners come."
Denny and I dressed in our sartorial best.
We were more impressive than the rest.
All the folks heading there
didn't have a care, which I thought a sin.
Denny, of a more mellow mind,
was not so judgmental; he was more kind.
He had a different approach brought on
by his appreciation of the thought-provoking roach.

Then I Met Madame Pele and Wahu

Madame Pele was perplexed
as her muscles she flexed, eager to take a walk
on this rock in the middle of the Pacific, the terrific Pacific.
Pele, with her flaming tresses.
Pele, with her flaming dresses.
She looked down—flame!
To waste precious fire is a shame.

Wahu, he prances, perchance he will see me
sitting quietly by the sea.
At night, only lava light!
While the water laps along the shore,
while the waves in the distance roar.
The ships go out to sea; the ships go out to see!

Still, the molten lava grumbles,
still, the molten lava mumbles
as down the mountainside it stumbles.
It oozes, tearing down the trees.
It oozes, bringing kahunas to their knees.
They know their gods are constructs of myth and lore,
created in the days of yore.

While the lava, flowing lava, spreading o'er the earth,
while the sea gives birth to the mountains and the islands
in the middle of the ocean, swaying, swaying motion.

Wahu continued on his jaunts
across the mountaintops, his haunts.
He carried a bone between his teeth.

He had found it underneath
a log sitting upon the mountaintop.
Sitting there, not a care.

Wahu is white with circles of black
around his eyes and on his back.
The pads of his feet are pink
as into the lava they sink.

I sat.
Waves lapping on the shore.
Was there more of Pele and Wahu
drifting through my mind, blind with fear,
of delusions so near, of illusions so clear?
The lava, up into the air it shot; it was hot!
It tore off the mountaintop!

Throughout the volcanic evening,
among the rocks and trees they went weaving.
Pele and Wahu continued to walk.
He would bark, and she would talk.

Madame Pele's Flaming Tresses

Madame Pele of the flaming tresses walked along the shore,
watching the volcano's lava roar
into the sky with twinkling stars.
The volcano aglow spit red-hot lava into the sky
as Madame Pele strolled on by.
Kahunas fell upon their knees,
yelling, "Madame Pele, help us, please."
Kahunas were filled with awe by the grandeur of what they saw.

Wahu

Wahu was strolling along the seashore.
The lava erupted high in the sky.
"My goodness," said Wahu, "the flowers will die."
Wahu was thinking; the lava did roar.
Madame Pele was mad, having a fit.
Kahunas were chanting, "Leave us alone.
Instead of cussing, give your dog a bone.
Quit all your fussing, quit having a snit."
The lava erupted, red in the night.
It poured down the slopes; it knocked down the trees.
Kahunas were frightened and down on their knees.
Wahu exclaimed, "What a glorious sight!"
Wahu, a ghostly apparition gay,
wandered alone in the midst of the fray.

The Lava Fields

The lava fields were so forlorn.
The lava rocks were gray and worn.
They stretched as far as the eye could see.

The volcano erupted, and the lava poured down
the sides of the mountain.
Everything and everyone that didn't get out of the way
were destroyed.
That is how land is formed.
The fields were the lava's home.

So I left Hawaii and headed east for San Francisco.
Trouble really began. Was it because I had taken
a lava rock from the lava fields and Madame Pele
was mad? Was It because I had no belief in God?
Probably the latter. However, I began thinking
of myself as "she, I" and "her, me." It was very
confusing to me and to anyone associated with me.

The Golden Gate

The sun was dipping to the horizon,
seagulls swooping over the Bay.
She kept walking. *Clip-clop* went her shoes.
Where were they heading?
It was dark in Golden Gate Park.
Evening stars appeared; it was late,
heading for the Golden Gate.
Walking, head pounding,
the thought of drowning slithered into her brain.
She became afraid, reaching the top, standing at the rail,
looking at the swirling water down below.
Jump! Hit the water with a thump and drown
far from ground.
Drown, water swirling all around.

Oh, Mr. Cop at the Top

Somewhere over the Golden Gate Bridge
I thought about making a splash, a crash,
Which "Mr. Cop at the Top" told me not to do.
Am I really so blue?
"If you will, call my mother or brother.
My father died with the help of a gun.
Were there six bullets or only one?
Pop, shot!
A bullet to the head, dead!
Russian roulette, you bet.
Therefore, guns I shun and abhor.
To save your life, I concede with all possible speed.
They should be delivered to those in need.
Oh, man-in-uniform,
Whilst all the cars did swarm, filling me with alarm,
All that noise in and out of my ears
Agitated my fear that I am really two.
There is I, and there is me; there is her, and there is me.
Confusing, don't you see?
Am I, I, or am I she?
But I am tired. Please take me home.
It is too late at night to roam around the town, no sound.
I need to sleep. Please take me home."

Dark Night of the Soul, Easter Morning 1974

The coffee had finished brewing, and the lovely aroma of Viennese cinnamon drifted throughout the apartment. I had developed a taste for more exotic blends, no longer just the black swill Dad and I used to drink in the early mornings when we sat and talked before the sun rose, and he went to work.

"I have not thought about him for the longest time. I wonder if I am oppressed."

I was hungry and was reaching for an apple when a voice thundered throughout my mind,

You are not normal!

The world crashed around me. I am not normal. What shall I do? What is wrong? What is wrong? I am so confused.

I lit a cigarette and watched the smoke rings drift from my mouth into the air. Voices whispered in my ears, strange voices I did not understand. It is Easter, and I should be going to church, but I am angry at how I have treated God and feel in total disgrace, so I would not be welcome at church.

I cannot bear feeling this way; I shall not stay this way.

I blew another smoke ring and coughed; a song appeared in my heart.

I hope when I die, God will take me to the sky.

I can drift from cloud to cloud, never being very loud.

I can drift from cosmos to cosmos, searching for the origin of fleas,

how they brought the dog and cat world to its knees

and travel through time at the drop of a hat.

I love to Google; I do love that.

My heart was lifted for a moment by the beautiful song I heard in my heart and then sadness.

There has been too much death in your young life. You are bereft by death.

Then the fog lifted, and the blue sky peeped out from the gloom. For a moment, my spirit was again cheered, not oppressed, inappropriately dressed, or psychologically stressed.

The Voices Stopped

The fire was burning in the pot as I put my Bible into the blaze
and watched it burn into ashes.
The smoke made a gray spot on the ceiling.
I sat on the floor, squatting on my heels
as I had learned to do in dance class,
Rocking back and forth, chanting,
"I have betrayed You! Strike me dead!
I have lived too long, wrong! Strike me dead!
I have lost my song! Strike me dead!"

The Bible blazed in the flames.
I continued rocking back and forth,
knowing God had heard me,
knowing my days were numbered.
But, the voices stopped!

Heartbreak

How did my heart break? How did it break?
It happened, I remember, when I was not awake.
How did it happen
in the gloom of a darkened, lightless hotel room
as moonbeams fell upon the floor?
How did it happen? I'm not sure.

Oh, yes, my heart, it broke in two.
I could not fix it, though I used glue.
It broke in two, it broke in three.
I need my heart to be, to be.
Without my heart, I have no hope of maneuvering
through the world, to cope.

Coping—a horrendous task!
I always carry a flask
of Diet Dr. Pepper
to cheer me up as it enters in,
enters into the place where hope does dwell,
propelling me out of the place known as hell.

Never Satisfied

"You are too fat; you are too thin."
No one ever likes the shape I'm in.
Should I eat more? Should I eat less?
No matter what I do, I seem such a mess.
I really should eat; I know I should.
I certainly would eat if only I could.
To eat seems a chore; to eat seems a hassle.
There are more important things
with which I wrestle.
The food won't go down; it gets stuck in my throat.
I would so like to eat, but it makes me choke.

Just yesterday the doctor got mad
and said I was selfish and should be glad
there is so much food available to me,
that I live in America, where food is almost free.
I got mad and called him a quack,
said I felt too skinny to go back to work.
I stormed out the door and flounced down the hall,
yelled over my shoulder to the quack and nurses all.
"Perhaps to the hospital I should be sent."
With this parting comment, through the door I went.

Later that night, I sat in the dark.
I thought and I thought about eating,
but the voices said, *Walk*.
I walked a lot now 'cause the food would not go
down, down my throat like it should, don't you know?
I walked day and night 'cause I could not sleep,
which was even worse than not being able to eat.

I figured as I walked from zone to zone
that all of my muscles had excellent tone.

God seemed quite distant, but I knew it was me
'cause God doesn't like for His folks to be hungry.
These voices will kill me—I know they will—
unless God provides me a magical pill
that will shut up the voices, send them far, far away,
so that once again I can sing, dance, and play.
I need this pill quickly because I am wired.
I am hungry and unbelievably tired.
Dear God, I do humbly pray that You will send me
this pill right away.

My Trouble Just Begun

Oh, Holy Father, three in one?
I rue the day my troubles begun.
They came, surprise,
Tumbling and stumbling before my eyes.

Voices! Voices! Think! Think!
Where, oh where, could they be hid?
Oh, of them to be rid.

Down, down it fell: thistleweed
survived the tumult of the seed.
Leaves float down like gossamer dust,
terra, terra, shades to the sound of rust.
Rust, loud and clear,
settled on the dirt so near. Help me, help me.
Help me, dear, so nearly, merely
the sound of thunder, tearing the land asunder.

Asunder, yes! Asunder, why?
Asunder sing out, laugh, and cry until I die.
Die! Why? You reply,
"Because I say so! That is why!"

Earth of Granite

Dirt and blood equal mud.
Dirt and glad equal sad.
Floating in the air, dandelion spores
don't need oars to maneuver.
But the wind, their friend, transports them.
North, south, east, west, they are welcome.
The thistledown floats, daintily spread
from one place to another, filling the air with powdery puffs.
I, too, would like to float upon the breeze
that causes living things to sneeze.

When I was given birth upon the earth,
the dandelions were giving their fragile spores
to the air, traveling where it seemed expedient,
traveling where they were sent.

When God first formed the planet,
He created lots of granite to hold the earth in place
as It meandered through the universe and space.
Oh, Mighty Spirit, let me hear it, what you have to tell
to make my brain and mind more well.

I Need a Beer

I remembered Lee.
It is good he got out of my apartment
before one of us killed the other.
I wandered back to the window;
the fog was lifting, nd the blue sky appeared.
For a moment, my spirit was cheered.
"I am thirsty," spoken softly, not screaming.
"Oh, dear, I need a beer, which I do not drink, I think."
I am confused, could shout, "Let me out."
My fear of heights has been compounded
on the sixteenth floor, where I have been impounded
for confusion of the mind,
being treated by medication, talk therapy, and Christianity
by a doctor kind.

I thought,
A cow
trying to jump over the moon, it will crash to earth soon,
where the flowers bloom as the airplanes zoom.
Across the sky they fly,
silvery tubes carrying souls, passengers and crew.

Then,
"Lights out, lights out!" boomed the guard's voice
as he marched through the psychiatric ward,
herding visitors out the door, locking it.
Click, click, click.

I was alone.

Such Grief

Psychotherapy

The very first time I saw my doc,
he made me think as I took a look at him
while sitting there in his plush, leather chair
with his silvery, flying hair.
It was plain to see he was much smarter than me.
Thus began psychotherapy.

It was San Francisco, 1974. I was sick to the core,
and what was more, I needed help, and for some
odd reason unknown to me, I knew it and sought
it. Enter Dr. Wang, a Southern Baptist Chinese
psychiatrist who understood that not only did I have
a mental illness but also a spiritual sickness. He took
it on himself to not only help me psychiatrically
but also to begin to repair the spiritual wounds. He
only had two weeks, but he began something that
continues to this day, June 26, 2019. Thank you,
Dr. Wang!

How Did I Get Here?

How did I get here? I do not know.
Was there an ambulance? Was it slow?
Did the sirens scream and wail
as they transported me from the jail?
For a fact. my life was a mess.
God saw this, a real live damsel in distress.

He got me to the sixteenth floor.
He got me a Southern Baptist doctor.
He need not do more.
Dr. Wang was small and sleek,
and moved around the floor so quick.
He gave me a shot and said,
"You should be thankful you're not dead.
But cheer up. Things get better, I always say,
when the sun shines down on a brand-new day.
After a day or so, you will not scream,
and all this will seem like a dream.
A confusing one, if I do say so.
Rehabilitation will be slow.
Do not get discouraged, do not get depressed.
Put on fashionable clothes when you get dressed.
Eat your meals, and smoke if you must.
When you get better, you'll stop smoking I trust.
Now, go to sleep and enjoy a good dream.
For goodness sake, please do not scream.
The other folks here need their rest.
Try real hard not to be a pest."

Place

It came as quite a shock to me to be inside this place
because to "polite society," "mental" is a disgrace.
Mental, yes, it is a state
of confusion and undo stress.
To be quite truthful, myself was a mess.
A mess, yes, a mess I must confess.

The walls were white; the doors were bolted
so we could not escape, so we would be halted.
There were no pictures on the walls.
They were so very bare.
It was hard for me to credit
that I was really there, that I was really there.

God looked down, inclined His head, and said,
"I must not hover! I must not smother
that little spark of genius that abides down in the interior
way down deep inside!"

One day Doc came. There had been rain.
The day was dark and gloomy.
The room in which I lay my head
was spare and not so roomy.
But it was all I had. I was too sick to be sad.
Doc looked at me and said,
"I think you need to get out more.
It is not helpful to stare at the door.

It is not helpful to glare at the door.
so follow me, and we will see *Star Trek*
with all the others whom you should meet.
Whom you should greet.
They all have a story, a history.
Why they ended up here is still a mystery."

Grace

"Oh my," I cried, looking upward from my bed.
"Why am I not dead?"
The sky looks odd as seen from behind bars
It looks black-striped and tired.

"Oh my," I cried, looking upward from my bed.
"Why did I not die? Tell me why!"

Doc's next job was really hard—
to make me gain some weight.
So this is what he said,
"You can eat, or you are dead."

I don't know why I had no reply.
God's grace descended upon me
before I was gone.
So I ate!

Space

He wrapped his air around him; he slid off into space.
I never really saw him; I only saw his face.
I never really knew him. I will tell you why.
He was just my doctor, and he taught me not to cry
Unless the circumstances warranted it.

He wrapped his aura on his head. Always did he wear it,
even into bed. He absolutely would not share it.
He was a most miraculous doc.
He even got me out of shock!

Lucy and I and Doc

One was wearing terrycloth slippers, and the other was wearing
Frye boots.
Clip, clop, they did not stop.
On down the hall—one tall, one small—
into the office of the doc.
They had made up their minds to buy new clothes and shoes.
They had the blues; they needed new shoes.
"Doc," they both did say,
"can we go shopping for new clothes today?"

"Girls, there is no way I will let you go outside and shop until you
drop.
But you have some money in your account. It is not a great amount.
I will send Nurse Melissa to look.
She will bring you back some slacks and a sweater.
Does that make you feel much better?"

"Thanks, Doc," they did both reply.
"You are a most splendiferous guy.
You give us such good advice, and you say it oh, so nice
that we cannot take offense.
You totally, totally make good sense.
We are not dead! You told us we must eat!
We must gain some weight! That must be our fate!"

I said, "I would like a sweater of red
That slips easily over my head.
Lucy would like a sweater of blue.
She is a French lady through and through."
Lucy piped up and said,
"I must confess, our hair is a mess, a problem we must address."

Doc replied with twinkling eyes,
"Girls, I must admit you surprise me.
You both seem more well off. In fact, you seem a little buff.
So we will address the way you look and get you up to snuff.
For now, that will be quite enough."

We gave shouts of glee, jumping up and down.
Twirling around, yelling, "Oh, look at me."

My Heart, It Broke

My heart, it broke, it broke in two.
What, oh what, is a girl to do?
It broke into pieces as it fell to the ground,
some pieces square, some pieces round.
Why did it break? Who can say?
Perhaps it was destined to be that way.

I silently stood and watched it fall
and wondered gently, *Is that all?*
It hit the ground and turned into mud.
It hit the ground; it bled and bled,
just like the old-timey poets said.

When it hit the ground, it turned into mud.
A compound, a mixture of dirt and blood.
Mud! A compound, a mixture of dirt and blood!

God Is Good

Oh, little dust mote, on a sunbeam you float
in front of my eyes! Are you so wise
that you know what my doctor will say
to help me chase the blues away?

"Miss Goin, you seem depressed.
Not only that, but your brain seems stressed.
We need to find you something to do—new—
to occupy your soul, something interesting to do.
I suggest you learn to drive, and in the process, stay alive.
Driving is interesting and ought help to focus your thoughts.

"The blues are not humorous, nor are they glamorous.
Don't sit and think about problems.
The best way to solve them is to occupy your mind
with new endeavors of a positive kind.

"Besides, you will need to get to the airport,
and in the country, that is the only means of transport.
Driving is fun and essential it be done.
So learn to drive and get a car.
It will get you here and there."

No ifs, ands, or buts.

The doctor agreed, and the airline concurred,
that to eat is to live; good health it can give, and
to the alternative, it is preferred.
It makes your nails longer; it makes your hair stronger.
Besides, it is fun to fill yourself up.
Do not eat more than your stomach can store
because that leads to fat, and we all know that is wrong.
No matter the reason, no matter the season,
fat in the airlines is not so pleasing.

Moderation in all things, as we all know.
Eating will help you grow.
Matter evolves from condition to condition.
It acquires mass, and it takes up space.
It gives you an edge in the evolutionary race,
a theory, quite popular, among the herd,
although we know you were created by God.
Many would disagree, but we do not care.
We think what we want, and we learn to share.
So eat up now; enjoy your crackers and dip.
When you get on the plane, there will be dinner to eat,
which will add to your hips.

> That was the end of San Francisco. Dr. Wang told me
> to contact Dr. Fowler in Richmond, Virginia, who
> told me to contact Dr. Lebensohn in Washington
> DC, which I did. So in June,

Then
The door opened, and there was a little old man.

I almost forgot my plan, and I almost ran.
I would like to get well; that was my plan.
This was too scary! But
I had to stay, not run away.
I was in

Ziggy's Room

It was a dreary, dreary day
in the merry, merry month of May.
My mind had been very far away.
I was sick and cold,
Not too terribly, terribly old.
Into the hospital I did go.
What would happen, I did not know.
I spent two weeks in the psychiatric ward,
Having been sent there by the Lord.

Doctor Wang was my doc.
Schizophrenia gave me quite a shock.
When I got out, he recommended
I seek psychotherapy.

So one fine day in June of 1974,
I dragged myself through Ziggy's door.
I was skinny, and my hair was a mess.
I was dressed in a pantsuit, not a dress.
I had made it myself; it was blue, and I was too.

Ziggy was sitting there,
Quiet and peaceful in his leather chair.
He had white and wild hair.
Me, he did not scare.
I knew he needed to hear the truth.

I was living proof of the deadly effects of
sickness of the mind.
Ziggy and Dr. Wang were kind.

"Miss Goin, so nice to meet you. I am Dr. Lebensohn. Please step
into my office. Why are you here?" he enquired, looking deeply into
my eyes.

I babbled, unable to stop.

The Electric Zone, the Electric Zone

of broken memories appears often as it pleases.
It teases and teases, leaving one to wonder and ponder.
Pondering on and on about such existential stuff
as, "when is when," and, "enough is enough."
That kind of stuff can be tough
to contemplate until it is late at night,
when the moon goes cruising, providing light.
Late at night, considering the whys and wherefores
of a life filled with strife, considering the short life of a duck
who is shot. Out of luck! His life comes to an end
as into the cosmos he blends.

The voices, the voices, where have they gone, the voices?
Here we are in the Electric Zone.
Please be nice, and give this girl a bone
to chew and bite and spit so as not to have a fit.
The Electric Zone is new to me,
but in actuality, it has existed throughout history,
probably throughout eternity.

> Dr. Lebensohn gave me oodles of good advice for
> living a meaningful life, including true love of
> God, art, music, dance, exercise, socializing, and
> watching my weight.

Matisse and Me

Not determined, nor is it fate
that I should paint every day.
I discovered the brush; it gave me a rush.
Something firm and new to learn.
A shining star to lead me far from my strained brain.

Matisse and me, we have in common the white expanse,
what to do and which color or hue?
What line goes here, what color goes there?
The line, the color, the shape form a map
upon which the colors can sink.
nor do we blink while your eye is passing by.

My brain pounded in my skull, forever focused.
My DNA! My way!
We like our surface flat, outlines in black and other colors.
It has occurred to me that painting is a mystery
as are the many sounds of music, or *mewsack*!

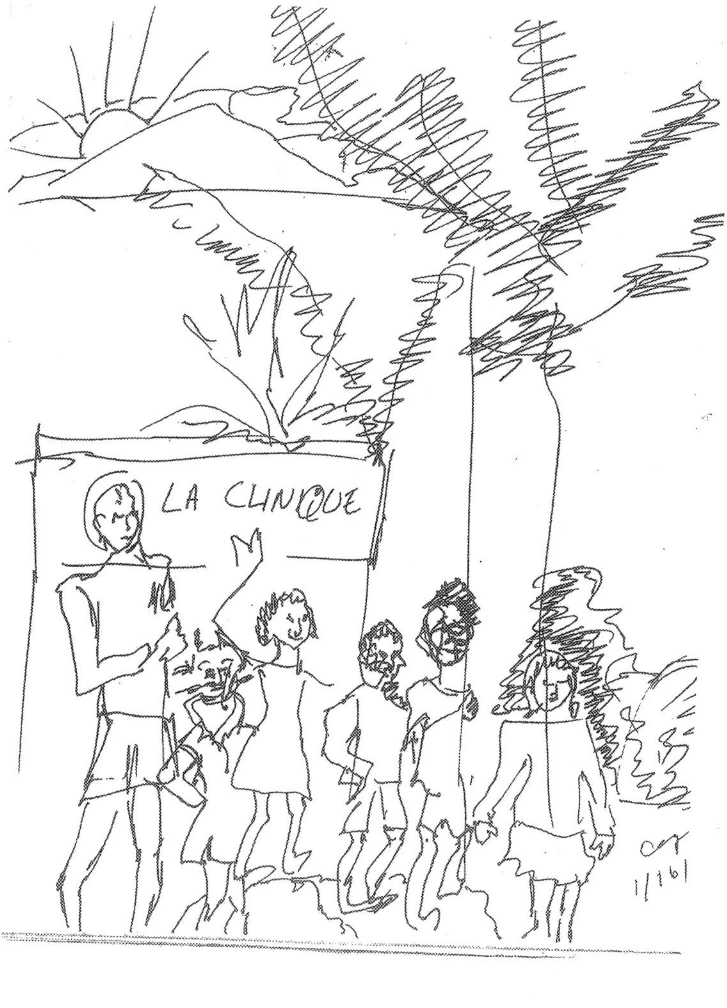
LA CLINIQUE

Gosnéde
nname

An Essay on Dance

Dance, most stimulating
to most societies in most times.
Sometimes considered sinful.
Phrasing is important, the use of the breath.
The hand flows in conjunction with the breath.
Exhaling, the line shoots out tastefully and accurately.

Being a flower petal is exhilarating,
better than the evening news.
Reacting to the sun and rain
Takes away the pain of grimness of life
in this big, bad world of strife.

Thinking this evening of a stretch.
Don't hurt one's self
whilst doing difficult moves, whilst one grooves.
Weeping with symmetry is therapeutic for me.
Asymmetry is more of a stretch
For this misguided, ungraceful wretch.

Fascinating to me is to see symmetry.
Motion, emotion, commotion, essence of devotion.
Sitting on the floor in touch with one's core.
Tomorrow, muscles will be sore.
To be expressive, that's what one does this for.
The art of making dances fluctuates as one prances,
surveying the audience with stealthy, subtle glances.

Symmetry, telemetry, psychiatry all appeal to me,
eevealing the inner shape of me, not descended from an ape.

Apes, trees
don't put much stress on their knees.
They are congruent, if you please.
Dancing, thinking, *It's not clear why I'm here.*
My back is old, and my hips are cold.
My brain is made of gray matter.
"Dance, dance, dance," it chatters.
When I stand up, I'm bent a bit
because of the stiffness in my hips.

One body appears, and then two.
More symmetry than three,
less appealing to you and me.

Being a flower is more appealing
than watching the evening news.
Reacting to the sun and rain
takes away the pain
of the evening news, full of horror and the blues.

Good Lord, I Am Sick

Click, click, click so quick; Good Lord, I am sick
Tell me why, before I die, You sent me two psychiatrists.
Or was it three? The best of the bunch
'cause I needed help would be my hunch.
My brain whirled, *Thoughtless, lawless,*
Retain good if you would.
Goodness! The room whirls, the flower swirls
nside the flower container in which it is placed,
Not like me, disgraced.

"Disgraced, Dr. Lebensohn," I said, slowly returning to the "real" world. "Yes, Dr. Lebensohn, I am in total disgrace."

"You will get over it," he said, reaching up to the second bookshelf from the top, placing his hand on one of his volumes.

"You know, Dr. Lebensohn, when I have insomnia, I stay up all night writing my book, which is about you," I said, a smile on my face.

"Why, that is thoughtful and wonderful. I hope you have made me a sympathetic character." He glanced at his watch. He was tired. He was well aware of his advancing years, and sometimes his heart felt weak. He felt hungry, but

He was proud! He was thrilled.
He had not been bored.
His patient was emerging
from beneath a cloud.

"No children for you! Not even one! Absolutely none!

Other outlets can be had or hobbies if you must!
Not rust in the realm of material articles made up of particles,
particles which dance and glitter
as throughout creation they flitter,
landing on a flower to announce that men you must renounce.
They do you no good!
No matter if you think they could!
No matter if you think they would!
Please go slow on obtaining new dresses,
which contribute to financial messes.
You must circle slowly around the truth,
like around a tree with me.
Doing that gives one proof

of the One who is here,
of the One who is there,
of the One who is everywhere!

Yes, you should wear black wrapped around your body and soul
now that you are growing old.

"And when you feel faint, how quaint.
Just keep on standing.
Look to the floor and look some more.
Hold on to a chair; hopefully one is there.

"But perchance if you should keel over,
hopefully in a field of clover
accompanied by a dog named Rover.
A cat, Scout, is out and about.
He is not fat but is sleek and trim with a black spot on his chin.
You could learn a lot from him.
He is your friend, although in truth, aloof."

After giving all this advice, he once again glanced at his watch. It was 4:00 p.m., time to close up for the night and go home. He slowly arose and said, "Miss Goin, enjoy yourself at Toast and Strawberries. Remember, you do not always have to buy something. It can be fun just to look." They shook hands. Although theirs was a professional relationship built over many years, they had come to have love for each other based on a deep, mutual respect.

"I expect," he said, "if the truth be said,
you would rather not be dead.
So be an insomniac if you must.
You do take a nap, I trust?
If you have been up all night,
struggling mightily, trying to write."

She left the office. She stepped onto the brick sidewalk and proceeded to Rosemary's.

Rosemary

She headed down the street to Toast and Strawberries. Rosemary, the proprietor, was standing in the doorway, tall and beautiful with a gorgeous black Afro. She and Rosemary walked into the boutique. It was like a cave with jewels lying here and there, sparkling and twinkling.

"Hi," Rosemary said. "How've you been?"
"Fine," she said to this hardworking dame.

Rosemary said, "See you've been to your doc.
Now it's time to shop.
In this corner of the store are many more items of interest
To a discerning being, capable of seeing.
Here is what there is to see, tee-hee!"

"Rosemary, this necklace is a gem,
Capable of raising one's consciousness to rationalness.
Don't you think it looks good on me?
Just curious, don't you see?
Tee-hee!"

Going to Church

I stopped my senseless activity and listened. It was years since I listened to the birds, to the old owl who lived nearby. He was old and wise. It was nice to listen to him. I hope someday I will hear an owl hoot again.
The birds all sang; their voices rang.
Their trills bouncing off the clouds
Joyful and loud; they were proud.
Their feathers ruffled.
In the birdbath they scuffled.
Who would bathe first?
Who would quench his or her thirst?
The trees swayed in the breeze.
The sap surged upward through their limbs.
The trees were singing hymns.

Several hours later, sitting in church,
Mama Mia,
How did I end up here, ah,
In this place of mis-ter-e-ah?
Who is the lady next to me-ah?
Who is she-ah, Mama Mia?
An introduction, if you please.

I trust you know this lady well.
I do not wish to end up with unwise friends in hell.
That would be the pits, worthy of never-ending fits.
Please, dear God, here I sit.
Help me choose my newest friends,
People who grin and smile in their hearts
In the presence of the One who inspires

Awh! Awe! Aw!
I hope I may see Him in the land
Where one wishes to be-ah,
In the Land of Mis-ter-e-ah.

Suddenly, throughout the church thundered the organ. The sound of "Great Is Thy Faithfulness" permeated the entire sanctuary. The choir and congregation joined their voices to that of the grand organ. I stood there speechless, enthralled by the lovely, majestic music. I must come again. Maybe next week.

Maybe next week, maybe next week
I will seek, I will seek!
It puzzles me, it puzzles my brain.
The old, sweet refrain is filling up my brain.

Help, Help, I Need Help!

Help, help, I need help!
What in the world am I to do with myself?
What in the world am I coming to?
First to go, I know, are my sacred cows
from the past and present nows.

Late July, sitting in my doctor's room,
trying to concentrate; what is he saying?
Oh, yes, I remember.
"Miss Goin, your life is a mess.
You're under duress and have a choice.
You must push forward or lapse into the backward mode.
You must put your brain to the ultimate test.
Press forward or eternally digress, not rest."

Had it been forever like this?

My brain had been under a tremendous strain, that was plain.
Something clicked, click, click, click! The brain was tricked
into thoughts of long ago, when time was slow, long ago.

Something went clack, clack, clack, clack.
No turning back. Bridges were burnt, new habits to be learnt.
Proceeding along the way, every day.
Something went clack, clack, clack, clack!
The doctors cut me no slack!
I knew I must do whatever was in accord
with the dictates of the Lord.

Four ladies sat with her, eating lunch. Or was it dinner?
No matter, it was a winner.
Little potatoes swimming there
between the sausage and onions.
The ladies were glad they had no bunions.
A glass of champagne in a sparkling glass
to cheer the heart of any lass.
Emptied the mind of anything dark
turned the dinner into a lark.

After I finally quit smoking, I gained twenty-six pounds in several years, and the doctor had a fit. "You must lose this weight. It affects your heart and even leads to diabetes."

Could It Be?

Is my fate to be fat? Is that to be my existence, or is it just resistance?
Is my heart duplicitous in the extreme, or is this all part of a dream?
As Weight Watchers said when I joined that fall,
I, too, can be skinny although not tall.
Unless I get rid of these unwanted pounds I will probably be dead,
In the ground earlier than need be. Tee-hee!

My clothes won't look good as I wish they would.
They won't hang and drape on my shape
As from a clothes hanger.
Eating won't be much fun if I can't cook.
Mindfully munching each bite at breakfast, dinner, and lunch.
Crunch, crunch, crunch!
Oil sizzles in the pot when the temperature is hot.
Little morsels brown, turning tender, making me slender.
Thank you, Weight Watchers, for your help
In making me svelte.

Fat Melts Away

"Oh, frabjous day. Calooh! Callay!"
Watch the fat melt away.
Where it goes is a mystery
unbeknownst to you and me.

Does it disappear down the drain
And head for the gutter in a torrent of rain?
Or does it go into the earth,
my disappearing girth?

Weight Watchers has added mindfulness
Into the life of stress, into a life of stress.
Weight drifting away, leaving me sleek and fey.
Hurray!
"Oh, frabjous day! Calooh! Callay!

Note: "Oh frabjous day! Calooh! Callay!" is from
the poem, "Jabberwocky" in *Through the Looking
Glass*" by Lewis Carroll.

Free Style

I have been following Free Style for a while,
and my weight has stayed the same—no loss, no gain—
which thrills me to my core, my heart.
Weight Watchers, so smart.

"How can that be?" you ask of me.
I do not know why it is so.
Could it be micronutrients? That makes sense.

But I am quite delighted
that the system works and doesn't hurt my soul,
which is old.

I Need a Coach

How I lamented when I consented
to never-ending therapy,
which helps me to forget Lee.
Which helps me to remember He
who has led the way from then 'til today.
I headed right one night, or was it twilight?
I took the uphill approach for which I need a coach
I can approach.
Yes, indeed! I need a coach,
which, dear Doc, is you.

I sat in the waiting room scene reading a magazine.
A glossy, shiny book of style while waiting for a while.
Then the door opened a crack! No turning back!
I ought, I thought, *to think of how to start a conversation*
with my gentlemanly doc.

"Hi there, Doc! How do you do?
I have missed you since last we met
and contemplated the history of the church,
which you condensed from the past to the present tense.

"Where am I in the flow of time?
How do I make my life rhyme?
The days long ago are forgotten mainly because they were rotten.
The memories which have returned
indicate how I have learned to act "normal,"
indicate how I learned to act formal."

Our Last Meeting

Eat lots of good food, get lots of rest.
Do not get discouraged, do not get depressed.
Always, always, always be fashionably dressed.
Exercise is a must; fresh air is too.
Following these rules will be beneficial to you.

Do not give up hope; don't use liquor and dope.
They will interfere with you trying to think.
They might bring you back to the edge of the brink.
Always, always, always, please take your pills.
They help you cope with myriad ills.
Always, always, always, please take your pills.

Try not to hide from people every day.
For good mental health, you need to sing, dance, play.
A job that is fun is of immeasurable worth.
Try to keep working as long as you can on this earth.
Put God at the center, and try not to hide.
He and your new psychiatrist will walk by your side.

> "So Miss Goin," he said to me at our last session
> after almost twenty-five years (he was retiring at
> the grand old age of eighty-nine), "I wish you the
> best in the future. I must say I like your orange hair.
> Most becoming to one with your temperament and
> coloring. Oh, goodness, our time together is up." As
> he said this, he arose, walked over to me, and took
> my hand, helping me rise from the chair. He walked
> to the door and out onto the street with me.

We both drew a deep breath and looked at the sky. We saw the storm clouds receding to the north. We were now in a box that had no top, or perhaps we were in a sphere. Going where? Not a care!

Ah, Relief!

The last section of this book begins with my cleansing of the soul in the Jordan River in Israel on December 19, 1999. It began a new century and a new me.

Baptism

I was baptized in the Jordan River.
It was cold, and I did shiver.
It was December 19, 1999, a day sublime.
The pastor said, "Hold your nose,"
As under the water I goes.
It was cold.
It cleansed and purified my soul.
I was old.

A Psychotic Break

I had a brutal psychotic break
once upon an age,
when nervous and mental breakdowns
were groovy, all the rage.

Recovery took up huge amounts
of thinking due to ire,
which mattered not to who or what.
It depended on your "fire."

The fire that burns way down deep within.
It started up when the doc said,
"Being a woman is no sin!
Be thankful you're not dead."

It always seemed way down deep within
that being a woman was a sin,
that something was lacking
way beneath the skin.
Your bones are frail.
Your brain is smaller.
Needless to say,
you are not taller.

It never did occur to me
that for me, there was a reason.
For each and every tumultuous season,
there was a reason.

I discovered I had a "dilemmer"—
whether to be fat or
whether to be thinner.

So here I sit,
not having a fit.
Here I sit
and sit and sit.

Dear God, thank You for the hope.
No longer will I mope.
You give me hope.
Lovely, lovely, lovely hope.

I Thought and Thought

I thought and thought.
I ought to do what is proper.
That is how you prosper.
So I though some more and more,
'til truly, truly my brain was sore.
Bells and whistles disturbed my brain
constantly, insistently
funneling into the now.

I knocked persistently at my brain,
saying, "It's going to rain,
which will modify my pain."
I really enjoy being sane
while sitting in my rocking chair,
rocking here, rocking there.
No pain!
Improving my soul, which is getting old.
Going where?
Not a care!

Day Is Done

Sinking slowly, lowly
into the ocean full of motion.
A man steps out of his car
and his wife, the love of his life,
steps out on crutches.
She clutches her crutches
and munches on an orange and white crab
caught that day while swimming on its way
by nets full of holes,
catching bodies, no souls.

But do we? Have souls?
Sometimes it seems the answer is no.
So which way should we go? Howling in the dark?
Hark! Hark!
Seagulls squawking, prancing, walking
along the concrete path.
Could it be they laugh?

The sun sinks and slinks into the water.
Is it a son, is it a daughter?
Sinking, sinking into the water.

Water full of waves and watery graves.
It sinks into the drink, I think.
I think, you think,
he/she/it thinks.

Inferior Interior

Myself, the interior, inferior,
not to mention the exterior.
I ask my heart why I'm not so smart,
not so intelligent, is that relevant?
Empty, oh, so empty! The wind moans, the wind groans.
It's cold, I'm old.
My marrow doth object
to the chill penetrating my bones.
I am alone!
Most of my family is gone,
and I keep wandering on alone.
My constitution is strong.
Thought is what you are.
I have traveled thus so far.

Listen, the birds sing about the worms
they caught for lunch, a carnivorous bunch.
But back to my earlier intention
about inferiority prevention.
Go deep inside the soul, and bring up songs of joy.
Bring hilarity to me, sing!
Inferiority long ago departed as simply as it started,
leaving a hole in my heart,
Which after many years, healed, departed,
as though it was never there.

It Was a Slippery Day

It was a slippery, slippery day.
Nothing was going my way.
Where am I? Where can I be?
It seems I have two feet
whereas I thought I had three.
Where can I be,
the other two or three and me?

I knew

1. Deep in my heart
    is a God from whom I can never part.

2. Deep in my mind is a God who is kind
    to me and the other two or three.

The Grand Display in the Sky, March 28, 2012

Ooh, la-la.
The sky is really cool.
The planets and the moon
aren't lined up this way often.

An extracelestial sight,
lights shine against the background
of the sky, midnight blue.
Twinkle dots, twinkle spots.
"Hallelujah!" shouts the Lord.
"I arranged this conjunction."
I was not bored.

The silver of the moon calmly lights the sky.
To the right is Venus, and Jupiter is hanging low
in the air.
This conjunction is quite rare!
The night is cold, midnight blue spread across the sky.
Trees sway first this then that way.
Orion glows to the left.
The stars sprinkle sparkle dust,
falling to the earth, falling to the earth. Not rust!

My Lean, Gray Shadow

My lean, gray shadow with me do walk.
It does not talk.
It is quite happy and does not squawk.
It is a blend of black and white.
It does not walk with me at night.
Depending on which side the sun is on,
it is either short, or it is long.
When I go out, it goes with me.
I hope It is mine throughout eternity.
Sometimes it runs ahead of me.
Sometimes it is on my side.
When night falls, it does hide.
When it is ahead, it is tall.
On my side, it is small.
Does it think? Does it dream?
Does it drink coffee with cream?
My long, gray shadow with me does walk.
It does not talk.

I was doing a yoga class, lying on my back with my
legs up the wall, when without warning,

Changes Deranges, No. 1

Was I downside up or upside down?
Were my feet on the ceiling or on the ground?
I was confused; was that because
I didn't know where I was?

The lights all glowed above my head.
The fans whirled around. Was I alive, was I dead?
Where were my legs? I had forgotten.
I was, in general, feeling rotten.

Dana appeared; she appeared forlorn.
"Are you here, or are you gone?
Please come back if you can.
Disappearance is not in our plan."
I circled around for another second.
Back in the studio, I reckon.
I took a trip. Where did I go?
Hours later, I still don't know.
"Dana, I have been dislocated!
Honestly, such occurrences are overrated.
Best left to the overeducated."

Changes Deranges, No. 2

Highly-rated to the uneducated
is the search for more as they head for the door.
"Pills for the ills," so goes the modern chant.
Or is it a rant?

A drink in the morning isn't too alarming.
But you can't continue the rest of the day
although some may disagree with me.
A drink for your soul is good as you grow old.
But when you are young and dumb,
A drink in the morning is alarming.

What can I say about today
And the way it has run its course? No remorse!
I have thought as I ought of all the things I've bought
And how they clutter up my space and mind—thoroughly unkind.

Changes Deranges, No. 3

Illegal, immoral,
but oh, so much fun.
It's truly disgraceful
the things I have done.

Perversely I did them
with a heart full of glee.
And they each and every one
backfired on me.

Changes Deranges, No. 4

Self-esteem, a dream of a bird flying by,
feathers falling from the sky.
A plane, a silver streak, gallivanting o'er the creek
where the fish repose.
Gaseous fumes infiltrate my nose
and dirtify my clothes, which are a mess
due to schizophrenia, I guess, of the paranoid variety.
From which I would like to escape.

Misery engulfed me years ago, when time seemed slow.
Not like today, it gallops away.
What ensued, the follow-through, was a question:
"What would you like to do?"
The question was perplexing, vexing, and hit a nerve,
causing me to swerve, heading in another direction.
One in which I was a child of God; how odd!
And one in which there was a reason for being here.
It is clear. Self-esteem.

Self-esteem! Even one drop makes coffee taste better
no matter the weather.
Self-esteem has overtaken me; free at last!
What a blast!

Changes Deranges, No. 5

Help me, Lord, what should I do
before my days on earth are through?
Before I pass away and see the end?

I'll float about upon my cloud,
playing music very loud.
I'll say a prayer floating from here to there,
spreading Your Word of hope.

"Trust in the Lord," that's what I'll sing,
"and He will bring happiness to you."
That's what He'll do.
I'll go on tour, where I'll endure
loss of life from this world of strife
and shall have fun when my new life has begun.
I'll wear celestial clothes made from golden thread
when I awaken from the land of the dead.
My harp and other instruments
will make me content, and my singing will be good
as I float from one to another neighborhood
and meet the other members of the band
in this glorious, celestial land.

And we shall sing, bang, toot, and strum
upon stringed instruments, flute, and drum.
A silver flute instead of gold upon which I'll toot.
And never again be old,
but eternally young and bold.
Which really appeals to me.
Tee-hee!

Changes Deranges, No. 6

The world appears colorful to me.
Or am I two or maybe three or four or more?
I'm split in two; what shall I do?
It's discombobulating to be dissipating
and even evaporating into drops of morning dew.

When I began to explore the way to sanity,
the door through which one must trip
if one wants to be hip and pulled together,
no matter the weather.
Paranoia was a surprise and filled me with what?
What indeed did I see?
What indeed pestered me?
Was it an alien from a ship way out there? Where
the planets and stars often collide
as through the cosmos they do ride?
Lufti from Mufti (my imaginary friend), who has been with me
from beginning to end, has pointy ears and greenish skin.
He's a friend who talks to me when I am mad/sad/glad,
and walks with me throughout the day
in every direction, in every way.

As does Wahu, my imaginary dog,
who is friends with imaginary Frog
Frog, he croaks, and Wahu, he barks
as we meander on our walks.

I rarely tell Doc about my chums
as in his office we attempt to discuss my disassociated brain
and consider how to appear "sane."
For those of a more conventional mind and brain
know to come in from the rain,
while my chums and I consider why to fly!

Yes, Indeed, I Hear You, Doc

Yes, indeed, I hear you, Doc.
As you know, I've been in shock, laden down with fear,
not having power, love, or a sound mind.
God's way is clear,
not disturbed as reported, clear as can be.
God's way makes sense to me.
God's way gives me hope.

At this juncture, my heart craves a joint,
Which is not in favor, legal, or affordable, but should it ever be,
there will not be so much mental misery
and sorrow of the thinking process.
Ah, yes, I regress to the time
I used to spend talking with "him."
Ziggy, I mean, the second doctor on the scene.
He sat there in his leather chair,
rows of books behind his head.
Most of them he had read, which impressed me.
I chortled with joy; he had the mind of a man, not a boy.

I confessed I was a mess, sick and tired to the core.
Voices deep inside pierced to the center
of all I beheld in a time long ago, the past.
So into my mind was cast a tiny, silvery ray of hope.
He knew I could cope.
He will forever be in the center of me.
He taught me how to think, I think!
At least I am not sick and have hung onto the present.
A modern Miss he did not "dis."

PS

It is spring; I must be mowing.

The dandelions and grass are growing.

Spring is showing its myriad colors.

Magical to behold; on the beauty of nature I am sold.

I love more as I grow old the things at my core.

My brain is no longer in pain, a wondrous gain.

Why I Like to Dance

I recently attained the distinction of having finally arrived at the beginning of "old age." Not "great old age," merely old age. There is a difference.

Arthritis in my left knee. Many of my friends have this disgusting ailment in their fingers, elbows, wrists, backs, and so forth and so on. All these areas cause great pain and lack of freedom of motion.

When this awareness came to me, I had reached what the US government considered old age. I had just attained the age of sixty-five. I wondered, *How could this have happened to me?* Horrified, I took more yoga and dance lessons. Yoga and dance stretches everything, and in general, makes one feel better.

But the fact remained, I had stiffness and pain in the joints!

For a dancer or would-be dancer, this is a truly horrific thing to have happen to oneself! The fluidity of the body's motions becomes compromised. What to do?

"Move!" a voice in my head thundered, followed by a murmur in the brain.

"Dance, dance," said my muse. "If you do not move, you will get creaky and out of the groove. It would behoove you to look around and enjoy seeing the agility of people who can still move gracefully and freely, who still have the beauty that is bestowed on those who have well-oiled joints."

But if the truth be told, I am grateful and thankful not to be confined to a wheelchair.

Walking in Paris

As I was walking down the street,
the drums were pounding out their beat.
Voices were wailing through the air,
wailing, wailing, "I don't care."

Chanting, chanting all the day.
Chanting the air is not warm.
The dogs will do no harm.
While vendors squat beside their rugs,
the homeless beg, and then they shrug.
They shrug because people pass them by,
not bothering to ask them why.
Why they lie beside the grate
with the wine bottle beside them?
There they wait.
What is the reason for their ennui?
I'd like to know; I'd like to see
what passes through their minds.
Do they even think about their plights?
They may be so sick they might
not even know they need a home
So they won't have to beg and roam.
Ladies bundled in layers,
hiding from the world,
Pushing loaded carts before them,
Giving insanity a twirl.
Squatting behind a sigh all the day
is an awful, awful way to live.

To live alone without a home or a friend
is an awful way to bring life to an end.

As I wander down the street,
behind me, still the drums
pound out their beat.

For nearly a year, I flew troops and equipment to Saudi Arabia and Kuwait during Desert Shield and Desert Storm.

Late at Night

Late, late at night,
our flight left Brussels
after dinner, beer, and mussels.

High in the night sky,
the plane so heavy.
Carrying a bevy of soldiers and freight,
we took off late.

White snow below;
ground covered with snow.
Flakes hit the fuselage of the plane.
Or is it rain?

PÉRE BRUNO

Then the year of 2010 came, and I went to Haiti on a mission trip. Wouldn't you know it? Haiti was devastated by a 7.5 earthquake, killing around 220,000 souls and destroying land and property. We were stranded in Terrier Rouge, cut off from communication with the outside world. Finally, as food and water were being depleted, we managed to escape. I wrote two poems and drew these illustrations, which is amazing as I was basically in shock. So were the people in these drawings.

Olde Man

Olde man sat in a chair and painted and painted.
His wife stood by his side and cried and cried.
A young woman languished in the sun and fainted, fainted.

The sun beat down upon the town,
upon the crowns of many souls.
Not cold, not cold.

Olde man said, "I'll soon be dead.
I'm made up of many a part,
also my heart."

His wife stood by his side and cried and cried.
What she was seeing pierced her being.
What she was seeing, what she was seeing.

Tremors

Tremors undulating beneath the ground,
Slithering up, slithering down.
World is shaking all around.
Birds all holler loud as they can.
Dogs all howl and run around.

Ground, it rocked, buildings rolled.
"An earthquake, an earthquake."
Shock, if the truth be told.

Helpless, lost control
As the firmament rocked and rolled.
Magnitude like 7.5, still alive.
Magnitude like 7.5.
Glad to be alive.

Thoughts on the Plane at Night

Have you ever thought, late at night,
That your mind is quite a fright?
Have you kept serendipity in sight?
We would all like to know
Which, oh, which way should we go?
As we dash from here to there,
And on occasion, stop and stare
At those whose sins do not coincide
With those which amble by our side.
With those unfortunates we tend to collide.

Here I sit,
Trying to remember what I ate
For dinner an hour ago.
I was hungry, don't you know?

I am trying to write,
Keeping my viewpoints clear and in sight,
About how one becomes a schizophrenic,
One whose imagination knows no lack.
The way to hell is paved, they say,
With brain cells which have gone astray.

Here I sit and ponder on
What in my life went wrong
That I should crack, a total nut
Who went to the hospital but
Found I could not prolong my stay
Because I did not have the money to pay.
Social Security was not here and would not

Show up until my sixty-second year.
Ziggy said, "You are not wired.
If you take your pills, you will not be fired.
Try to figure out what normal is.
If you do that, you will be a whiz.
Try, try each and every day."

I pondered work, I pondered play.
What was right, what was wrong?
How many sentences were too long
To hold the attention of the audience.
Should they be in the past, present, or future tense?

I painted and painted for all I was worth,
Trying to convey my ideas of life on this earth,
Wondering what went on in the minds of folks.
Upon what did they pin their dreams and hopes?

I, too, would pretend that I was normal,
Although in the process, I became quite formal.
It is difficult to pretend all the time
That you are sane and suave and urbane.

Dear reader, if you are so inclined,
Join me in this book of mine
As I try to explain how it all got started.
If you are so inclined.

Thanksgiving

Thanksgiving-time to me is going slow.
Schizophrenia in the flow, on the go.
To memorize a verse might lift the curse
Brought on by discontent, which won't relent,
and then, behold, while it is cold,
a little voice from deep inside my gut says, "Hello,
you seem much better than when last
I encountered you in the past."
In the past, could it be a touch of eternity
brought on by a man with green blood
which, when mixed with mud,
is a vibrant green last seen when I was a teen.

Lufti from Mufti, my favorite friend,
with the greenish-tinted skin and buggy eyes,
you come again! Surprise!

It's been many a year since last you were here.
Now I find you in my soul, a sign
my soul is growing old and no longer cares
If others share our way of saying, "Hello."

Winter Is Here

The sky deep blue, ink-like, intriguing.
Behold, Orion appears with his warrior gear.
His belt across his waist!
Following the sun in the nightly path it runs,
Sinking low beneath the trees.
It is winter! What, no leaves?

The sky, starry winter sky, the dark, dark sky.
And to the North appears the North Star,
Guiding us through the night, when there is not much light.
Snow blankets the earth.
Power lines hopefully stay in place; we will stay warm.
The blanket of white lays upon the earth.
No despair. Spring is coming; it's in the air.
The snow drizzles and giggles, the earthworm wiggles
As it burrows beneath the ground
As the earth twirls and whirls around.

As you can see, as my love of nature has resurfaced,
my poetry is more about nature.

Winter Poem about Snow

Crows flying, cawing, over the snow,
through blue skies, not sighing, no!
Crows sitting on a telephone wire,
contemplating flying higher.

The sun peeps through winter's brown trees,
entertaining the evening breeze.
Sparrows flicker up and down,
over the snow-smothered ground, no sound.

Squirrels and crows fighting for a grain of corn.
Bam, bam, goes the squirrel; crow flies up, gone.
Snow covered, white like the beams of the moon,
fills our souls, empties our glooms.

White—oh, so white—obliterates the light,
perpetuates our glooms.
Through the sky snow zooms,
zooms on a slant, quietly, not a rant.
Perchance moisturizing soil and earth
'til spring brings forth new birth.

Snowdrops, springing, thanks.
Walking, slush, the world has turned to mush
in a hurry to usher in the spring.
Throughout the heavens
songbirds sing, their voices ring.

Mr. and Mrs. Cardinal out in force
Must find food, have no choice.

Sunflower seeds fallen into the weeds.
Getting food is hard.
The birdfeeder is the most popular place in the yard.

Empty, empty space.
God's grace is enough.

Icicles through the Ages

As I have gotten older,
the world seems more magical
as the sun shines through
my window in the dawn
dancing before my eyes,
dancing sparks of fire,
flames rising, ever higher!
As I have gotten bolder,
the world appears more radical
as the moonbeams sparkle
through my window at night.
And as I grow colder,
slowed down by advancing age,
I've noticed for myself and my peers
warmth and light of the sun
are all the rage.

The Bird, the Worm, and the Butterfly

The bird was hopping on the grass.
"There are no worms," he cried. "Alas."
He was speckled, black and gray.
I had never seen a bird
dressed quite this way.

The bird with the speckled feathers
was different than cows,
with their variously colored leathers.

He said, "I have looked high and low.
Where, oh where, did they go?"
He was talking about the worms
which wiggle and squirm.
Worms are smarter than they look
or that we have been taught
in many a book.
They have learned to burrow in the dirt
to get away from birds,
so they will not get hurt.
They are so wiggly and a glorious brown
as they burrow all around underground.

The speckled bird, he thought and thought
about how to catch a worm.
If only above the ground it would peep its head,
then I would take a big gulp,
and he would be dead.

Although it is getting late,
it would make a great dinner,
the best I ever ate.

At that moment, the bird looked up
and saw a butterfly flitting by in the sky.
The bird, he thought with infinite glee,
That butterfly will an appetizer be.
The bird arose.
The butterfly, unconscious of the bird swooping down
from up above, did not realize his time was up
as he was heading for a buttercup.
The bird gulped him down.
He disappeared into the bird's stomach,
where he was secured.

The bird, with glee, landed in a tree.
The worm, beneath, gave a sigh of relief.

The Crows

The crows descend and sit upon tree limbs,
shouting out jubilantly their evening hymns.
The sky rings out with their, *Caw, caw, caw.*
People sitting on their decks clap their hands in applause.

The crows are sleek, and their feathers are black.
Of wintertime food they have no lack.
The other neighbors, disgusted by the mess they make,
get out their guns, no mistake.
The sky reverberates with the shots,
bullets hitting here and there, sundry shots.
The crows, to retaliate, take to the air,
evacuating—plop, plop, plop!

    A direct hit
onto the roofs of the vehicles.
Down through the sky, trickle, trickle, trickle!
How they aim so well is hard to know.
They do it fast, not so slow.

A Late Fall Evening

Golden-orange leaves
fall and sigh.
Clouds follow jet streams.
Huff, puff.
Wooly bear's stripes
tell of coming chill.
Blackbird flaps
his wings, breezes sing,
silver sparkles in the clouds.
Lots of them, a crowd.
Darkening clouds evaporate
like smoke pushed through a pipe.

When I Go Beyond

I hope that when I die,
God will take me to the sky.
I will drift from cloud to cloud,
Never being very loud.
Drifting from cosmos to cosmos,
Traveling through time
At the drop of a hat.
I love to Google; I do love that.

Winter and Snow

Snow! What can I say? It makes my tires spin, makes me slip when I go out for a walk, and it causes the heat and lights to go off when it weighs heavily on the wires lining the street. Sometimes it keeps me indoors, waiting for whatever the weather might bring.

But when it's just snowed and the world outside glistens with a coating of white and silver, joy rises in my heart, and excitement comes from watching the busy, hungry squirrels and birds at the feeder in the backyard. The trees bow down from the snowflakes resting upon their limbs and branches. The brown-ness of late autumn is covered by a comforter of new beginnings. But wait! A patch of blue appears. The sun peeps out in the sky, and I am pulled out of myself into a new and beautiful world.

There have been many long, cold days in my life, knocking at my door. I no longer pay attention to them. I keep on looking for those gorgeous patches of blue and the sun once again emerging. I make hot soup, put on my red, wool coat, and head outside to find the beauty of the new day calling me.

The End

Or as Omar Khayyam said to me in a voice one night (rendered in English verse by Edward Fitzgerald in the Rubaiyat, XV1)

Think, in this battered Caravanserai

Whose doorways are alternate night and day,

How sultan after sultan, with his pomp,

Abode his hour or two, and went his way.

And to sum up the story, this memoir, I thought this little ditty would be appropriate.

I am a schizophrenic of the paranoid variety.

That's why it's hard to fit, you see, into polite society.

I am a schizophrenic of the paranoid variety.

That's why I fit so well, you see, into inflight society.

Help, help, I need help.

My brain is tingling under my scalp.

About the Author

Catherine E. Goin is an old person with a young soul. After studying painting and dance at the College of William and Mary, she painted for fifty years until she introduced the flute, guitar, mandolin, and writing into her life. Catherine lives with her brother in a small town in Virginia. This is her fifth book.

Printed in the United States
By Bookmasters